EVERYTHING THAT CAN HAPPEN
POEMS ABOUT THE FUTURE

Note from the illustrator: For this book I decided to create series of scenes of the old town centre of my hometown of Bracknell, once a vision of the future when it was designated a New Town after WW2.

THE EMMA PRESS

First published in the UK in 2019 by the Emma Press Ltd

ISBN 978-1-910139-52-3

A CIP catalogue record of this book
is available from the British Library.

Printed and bound in Great Britain
by TJ International, Padstow.

The Emma Press
theemmapress.com
hello@theemmapress.com
Jewellery Quarter, Birmingham, UK

EVERYTHING THAT CAN HAPPEN

POEMS ABOUT THE FUTURE

Edited by Suzannah Evans and Tom Sastry

Illustrated by Emma Dai'an Wright

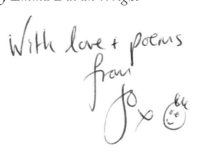

EDITORS' FOREWORD

How do contemporary poets imagine the future? Your answer is between these covers. There are many kinds of future in here, and versions of our world that are recognisable in differing degrees. Poets look forward in different ways: some anxiously, some with hope, and some with resignation.

Some look into a distant, apocalyptic future; some take the moment we live in and nudge it very slightly beyond what we know; all explore their feelings about the present. This book is full of energy, prophecy, humour, despair, passion, anger, fear and love. It is sometimes indecent. It looks unflinchingly into the darkness, at the brutality of human nature and the fatbergs of our shadow selves.

This book is profoundly humanistic. It understands how high the stakes are, whether the future in question is that of a single person or the whole of humanity. It is deeply concerned with the question *what is it to be human?* It has some surprising answers.

What this book does not offer is carefree optimism. In these times where both the planet and Western politics appear to be at melting point, that is not a surprise. What is surprising is how little the book touches on current affairs. We mentioned the Trump Presidency in the blogs we wrote to accompany the call for submissions. Our poets did not. There is no Brexit in this book.

Instead, the prophecies in this book are varied; there are robots and floods. There is cryogenic thawing, strange music and occasionally a glint of hope for the future.

Perhaps what the book reflects is not so much our immediate fears as the fact that the foreseeable future is, almost by definition, a frightening place. For one thing, it is going to kill you. Even more annoyingly, it favours those already on the rise as we project current trends forward. It is the place where our most urgent fears are played out. When we anticipate the future, it is natural to take the aspects of our own time which are changing fastest – the ones we understand least and find most alienating – and amplify them.

This book looks forward with trepidation, not cynicism; with a profound sense of human fragility and an intense engagement with life. It is full of mischief and full of beauty. It contains a spirit which, fortified with a little optimism could transform the world.

But because the future is unknowable, let us stick with what we know. This is a collection of poems which had the power to take us somewhere unfamiliar and make us believe in it. We hope you enjoy them as much as we have.

SUZANNAH EVANS AND TOM SASTRY
NOVEMBER 2018

CONTENTS

SECTION THREEE: A DIFFERENT KIND OF LIFE

SECTION FOUR: AT THE END OF THINGS

☙

SECTION ONE

THE FUTURE IS JUST A POINT IN TIME

To sit, conscious of occupying an arbitrary present, looking into the past or the future – this is a deviant act. It subverts our animal nature.

It creates a radical fiction: that the past and future are places we can imagine if not visit.

These places were never equals. The past has precedence. It has reproachful ancestors and heroes of improbable dimensions. It has a form.

The future has none of these. There is something disreputable about it.

counting

every ten seconds a wave breaks
      swirls up the shore
forty babies are born
      twenty into poverty, twenty people die
a hummingbird's wings beat seven hundred times
      lightning strikes the ground in a thousand places
ten thousand barrels of oil burn while the sun
      flings five million tons of matter into space
and the universe expands by ninety-two miles
      the next wave comes, drenching my boots

Mechanical Time is not the Creator's

after Franz Radziwill

A bird with broken mechanics clanks its cuck-oo.
An hour glass rolls across the highway like tumbleweed.
A grandfather clock skids down the stairs.
An ancient sundial is covered in moss.
A giant station clock rat-ta-tats along the tracks.
A clock with no hands washes up on the shore.
A magpie escapes with a watch in its beak.
A monkey finds a chain watch to play with.
A clock tower leaks unmeasured time.

Womb

I am looking at a tree.

I regurgitate my tea and the water rushes up into the tap. It's getting earlier and earlier. Soon, we are reversing around the Dordogne as summer flies unpick themselves from the windscreen.

Mum and Dad's ashes turn to flesh in Rotherham crematorium as they go back to exhaling cigarettes and un-watching Crimewatch in a series of bungalows. Meanwhile, at the Brazil World Cup, the London Olympics and the Boston Marathon, everyone is running backwards. Fewer and fewer people are tapping their computers which are getting slower and slower, as their modems get louder and louder. East London is getting worse. Camden Town is getting better. Canary Wharf is getting lower, Brixton is getting blacker. I go back to university, unmeet my husband, the millennium comes in an implosion of fireworks.

In Berlin, spray paint peels off the wall, liquefies, is sucked into a can. The same thing happens in New York. Suddenly, a lot of my friends are getting really small. They are stuffed back, scream-inhaling into the wombs of their scream-inhaling mothers. Somehow, I am still here and hair is being cut longer. The Beatles are back together and all their records are spinning backwards. Except for the ones with hidden satanic messages, which are spinning forwards.

Soon, my mother is pushed back into grandma's womb and women everywhere leave factories and start unpicking their knitting. Hemlines get lower and lower and dresses suddenly puff to a sheen as everything gets slower and slower, but there are still wombs. Marie Antoinette finds her head. Men wear wigs, then tights and Columbus or the Vikings lose America, the Mongols and Muslims and Goths and Christians and Romans retreat, retreat, cities disappearing, Cleopatra brushing off her make-up. Wheat fields grass over. Ceramics turn to clay, stone circles are dismantled, cave artists brush ochre back onto pallets and it's wombs and wombs all the way until the last few people hop back across the savannah, their arms getting longer and longer.

The trees welcome them back.

Future You

I'm delegating that task to future me he says, flipping his thick,
    dark fringe from his eyes
and leaning in for a sip of skimmed milk macchiato, no cake.
I picture Future Him.

Same carefully quirky cardigan,
thick-rimmed glasses, with just clear glass.
But Future Him is punching desperate numbers
into his ergonomic keyboard
gesturing spasmodically to the screen
muttering things like *how? how? fuck.*
Eventually he thumps the desk with his fist
looks over at Future Me in bewildered defeat.

Future Me is gorgeous. Future Me's hair is amazing.
Future Me has finally found a hairdresser
capable of sculpting her hair to the perfect pixie crop. Sassy
    and feminine.
Future Me smiles compassionately and shakes her pretty head.
Alas, even in the future a simple girl cannot understand. Poor
    Future Him.
Future Me twiddles the flash disk in the pocket of her dress.
A dress with pockets is a glorious thing.
And here in the future we all have them.

Yeah, I say. *Let future you work it out,* and shove the last bit of
    brownie in my gob.

Signs of the Times

It is an injustice
                flowing from
the future's poverty
of imagination

   (or so it seems
to the recent past)

that animals have only achieved a superintelligence
sufficient to play the keyboard
   hilariously;

that the most immediate use for a robot
is in a McDonald's; that AI

was clearly invented so as to sell me
a number of knockoffs of Dwayne 'The Rock' Johnson –
or else he
was invented to sell me knockoff AI,
and I cannot decide which depresses me more;

that smart drinks had died by the time I could drink;

and, for that matter, that I can enter
a shop purporting to sell me 'e-liquid'
and *not* walk out with a bottled swarm
of bleeding-edge nanomachinery

capable of scrubbing my cumbersome system
of all its organic sludge and leaving me
sparkling, disease-free,
and with maybe the lightest dusting
of superpowers.   A travesty

to be sure. But still,

we've got time. The culture in its petri-dish
quivers and multiplies.

It could still become a requirement
of any of my future CVs
to include some variations on a theme
of 'interning cyber-terrorist'

and here, a woman with a baby has passed
in the other direction to what, I assume,
is a shift at the corner Waterstones wearing what

are very clearly robotic shoes,
bristling with filament and hope
adapted for high-speed parenting
    and afterwards, antigravity
tap dance.

Once

John Keats scraped the dawn frost from his windscreen
left the engine running so the AC could heat up as he did the bins.

He was generally concerned about maintaining fuel efficiency
in his 1.6L family hatchback but accelerated hard to join the flow of traffic.

At the brow of the first hill he pulled over, brought to a halt by the thick yolk
of sunshine spread like tempera behind the black ink of a bare oak

so he turned the radio down and settled in to watch the golden orb
break across the county for a while. It silvered through a bank of fog.

In the next valley he had to stop again, this time in the car park of Burger King,
turning the morning DJ to mute to allow for deeper contemplation.

He was late for work and failed to deliver on time a report concerning the efficacy of direct marketing strategies for clients in the blinds and curtains sector

– a task which he thought of as throwing the dust of his learning into the winds of indifference – but John Keats did not allow small things

such as these to ruin what had been, until this point, a good day. Besides, as he wrote in the morning's first email, it will none of it matter a year from now.

To his crazy future eyes, looking coyly at the future

You will love tomorrow they say, bulging
with optimism, never still, ever shifting:

ambition red from seeing so far,
China white for the geopolitical bet,
imperial origin blue for all that he wants,
powder green for the fire under the present +1.

Motes in coltskin swirls emboss the air in front
of him, the patterns of belief he weaves,
before they straighten into the cord lines
we'll all follow, living on quantum wi-fi alone.

Oh but you want more than the world and time!
Sit down by Elliot Bay and think about this:
vision alone cannot change what's next;
and would you be kind if you weren't rich?

Divination

We knew everything, playing oracle on the carpet.
Saturdays crawled with our ladybird circus –
on the ends of our fingers, solemn as blood,
      we sent them to find our future husbands.
We let them trickle down
      our wrists into the birdbath
to see if they'd keep walking while we drowned them,
jealous of their easy flight

      from one shape to the next.
Now, like hanged men, we want to buy futures
and there's someone doing tarot at the end of Brighton Pier.
Stars are poking holes in the sky and the birds
are coming into roost. There's an airy clatter

      of cards falling into place
but stranger things are happening beneath our feet:
coppers chink through the boards
onto rows of starlings
stacking themselves like decks, noisy as a masked ball.
      We think fluke has something to do with wings
then remember whales, gliding
          despite the weight of all they know.
We watch the stragglers find their place under the pier,
      all the sea's dark spread ahead of us.

Feed the Fatberg!

'Joseph Bazalgette created a sewer system which he originally sized for London's needs of the time – he then doubled it to anticipate the future beyond.' Norman Foster

In denominations of London buses, it muscles
and frets at areas counted in Wembleys, fingering
Theatreland's fifth wall.

Needles and wads
matted, hard and soft, mushrooming
alive and static like coral. It groans for rank

nourishment – this anti-compost.
Let's provide it with gross matter from leg pits,
covert waste-pullings, grill trappings, goldfish, miscarried

matter, old porridge. It has its own scouring effect,
making a fisting, nudging procession
weaving a dense, greasing mesh,

mouthing in caverns, tonguing bricks,
hatching swarms, polluting rats. The stuff
below street level does not relish being drilled

into daylight. But piecemeal the invasion
is tenderly curated above. Feed with caution,
never after midnight, do not break the glass,

wear goggles and gloves if watering
or scratching a crust. For what has been freed
are the contents of us.

SECTION TWO

JUST AROUND THE CORNER

The future these poems imagines feels very close, perhaps a little too close at times. The floods are lasting longer, the storms are surging and those we love are talking about the world they might be leaving behind. These things are no less terrifying because we recognise them.

And what can we do to prepare ourselves, for this future that gets a little closer every day? Do we stockpile, adapt new technologies, or resign ourselves to this weird new world, one which looks a lot like the one we're living in?

Daughter

女儿，
你会继承我的语言吗？
你会安静快速地说话吗？
在初学语言时常常犯错
然后不断进步吗？
我倒希望你说话不那么害羞
当你有孩子的时候，写下关于他的诗。
你的姑妈快要和一个很棒的德国人订婚了，
你的爸爸，我，将会有个外甥女-
"双喜临门"。我正在写诗，
我也害怕未来。你会和我一样害怕吗？
你会找到另一种更简单的语言
去表达自己吗？我将拭目以待。

* * *

Will you inherit my language,
speak quiet and quick, trip
over words like paving stones
with our large feet and fast apologies?
I would rather you speak less shy,
and only write poems about your children
once they exist. Your aunt just got engaged
to a nice German man and your father
shall have a niece – "double happiness,"
and I am writing a poem and fearing
the future. Will you fear it the same way?
Will you find that some things are easier to say
in a tongue that is not your own? I will wait.

An unborn child wonders if it's worth it

They say the seas catfight by night,
that rabbling gales scorch huddled girls?
Well, toffee, Haiti howls, that's right.

Lizards and ladies stoned in deserts,
rows of heads popped by rocks in red little shocks?
Oh, poppet, the tongue that cocks will cop it.

And grannies and mice are vial mummies in cold countries,
mummies in others suck gun through their gums?
The choice, Lucy Locket, is yours to grace this earth.

Liver, cornea, lymph rotted from rust in water,
babies burping the expiration of suicide daddies?
Every little helps through WaterAid monthly, kiddo.

But the tremor of stars stirs furious lovers together?
Yes. Points and counterpoints horrify me.

And the migratory Brahminy kites swoon at Lake Chilika?
Pumpkin, most folk are wanting to flee.

Maybe I'll whistle to see who picks up my tune?
Weigh it up, petal, maybe we'll see you soon.

Gaza

We sat on the prom staring out to sea
when I read you a sonnet about Gaza.
We stayed quiet half a minute, until
you said *I fear I'll never live to see
the end of that. You may – but I think
it'll drag on for ages.* I understood
you were giving me permission for years
without you, making me fill a little life
after you've gone, hanging on
for Gaza to be solved, waiting
for no more boys to be killed
playing football on the sand.
We fell silent again, wanting Gaza
glorious and you here to see it. You. Here.

Worlds

again and again people ask
me about the words that
make up my language   and I
always say *they are not words*
they are worlds

the Gujarati word for country carries
a world within   and when my grandfather places
his wrinkled hand atop my head   tells me
he is returning to his *desh* for the winter
a world unfurls

a world of love and longing
of piggybacks across the ocean
of TB-stricken loneliness   pay packets
and passports   a world in
search of a better world

at the temple I hear
Om   shantih   shantih   shantih
tucked into this plea for peace
there are tides   energy
galaxies   and eternity
Shantih   peace for I
       Shantih   peace for us
          Shantih   peace for the universe

recalling my sister's wedding day
I tear up at *vidai*
what's that? I'm asked   and I
refuse to reduce the word to
'the final stage of a Hindu wedding
ceremony when the bride bids
farewell to her family'

       how do I say   all the
words of the English language
are redundant in the face of this
word   and no words can
contain the pain of this moment?

21

when the bride sobs into her
father's chest   she sees the
times he hushed a weeping
wound   sees the nights they
chased the moon together

and when she scatters rice over her
head   she hears her mother calling
up the stairs   hears the
stories that lulled
her to sleep

how do I say *vidai* bears
the contents of the life a bride
leaves behind   a world
forsaken in time?

again and again   people ask me
about the words that make up
my language   and I always
say *they are not words   they
are worlds*

Flood Defences

At first, despite the groundsman's pique, they tried
hybrid grass, *reinforced with synthetic fibres,*

opinion was divided, the bowlers loved it
but the green top was a graveyard for batsmen.

Next was a new drainage system, *Hi tec polycarbon,*
can drain 18,000mm/hour, the brochure said

but it was no match when the Severn burst its banks
for the fourth time that year. Visiting teams complained

about cancelled fixtures and how their fielders
had to share the pitch with wading birds,

away fans brought duck whistles and started
quacking the home batsmen out of the clubhouse.

Finally they declared defeat, pulled up the stumps
for the last time and bailed out to higher ground,

now the old pavilion doubles as a boathouse,
the weather vane's cricketer rusted

in a permanent drive towards the covers
where the abandoned roller's sunk in the mud.

River boats make detours to cruise the boundary,
moor up at The Last Man Inn, where punters can partake

of *the cricketer's traditional afternoon tea*
whilst viewing signed bats displayed in glass cases

and photos of the old ground in its heyday.
A handful of regulars sit on 'traditional wooden benches'

(made in a factory in China) and reminisce
about the good old days when rain didn't stop play,

while swans reach their centuries swimming between the creases.

Reef

They call this place a reef. Walk a few hundred paces
and you reach roads, buses, direction. There are

fields too, horses, a wooden fence opposite a church,
a wall where children line up each Sunday. Now, why a reef?

Maybe you'll recognise it. Maybe you'll spot the moment
a break in cloud filters through and fills

a dual carriageway, a school hall, an underpass.
Maybe you'll hear a plane turn over train tracks, bridges,

a supermarket car park
and you'll catch its shadow on the concrete,

its rattle, its wind in the leaves of birch trees
planted for colour. And maybe, just maybe you'll remember

the time water existed here, the time the horizon was the end,
the time stingrays passed in silence.

And – if you get this far – we'll guess
it was you. The first to unstick an eyelid, blink in the darkness.

Yes, you who told us to 'Come, come this way',
offering a hand and pointing towards the light, asking us to walk

when the sand at our feet was nothing but shells
broken and broken a thousand times.

The End of the End of the Pier Show

Call it The Titanic Spirit: tonight
we have a show to end all shows,
kicked off by our teenage xylophonist
performing 'Flight of the Bumblebee' blindfold.

Be dazzled as El Niño, East Anglia's premier
flamenco troop perform their showstopper routine –
testament to our belief in Victorian riveting,
balustrades and glitter balls.

Yes, we have stood by, watched struts
that held up Yarmouth's ice-cream shops erode,
waved goodbye to penny-slot telescopes
sloshed away in last year's high spring tide.

But your tears are now no longer enough
to resalinate the oceans – so tonight
let's raise the roof of the Cromer Pavillon:
Resist the Great Storm Surge!

It may be too late for the Andaman Islands,
but money raised from ticket sales
will help those forced to flee bungalows
on the English Riviera.

And if we become unmoored midway
drift out on this boardwalk ark to darker seas,
don't panic, ladies & gentlemen,
our Michael Barrymore tribute act is first aid trained.

Enjoy our award-winning stage hypnotist.
The house band – the King Canuters –
will play loud and long into the night,
as we sail on, towards uncertain morning.

Breaking the Curfew with Dangerous Friends

Tonight, they are back in town,
lipstick scrawled on mouths strong from saying *No*.
They make quick work of roadblocks – *lady, baby,
bitch, witch, slut* – snap them like tinder-sticks.

They sneer at ranked telephoto lenses, stare down
those who gloat at the tabloid mess made of their bodies.
They stride to each house and knock:
not to help with the dishes or change

nappies, but to rouse us where we slump,
fretting over the bills, the buckled marriage,
the dinner party menu of impossible dishes.
Not all of us hear them. Some crank up

the volume on the TV, some swallow
ourselves into computer screens. I ignored
them the last time they were here, laughed off
the warnings, thought of all the safe years stretching

out before me. This time my ears are cocked
for the gravel crunch of footsteps. I've slashed
the hemline of my skirt to show the muscles
I have built for running. My shoes are at the door.

In Case

A small book on mushrooms, field guide
to foraging; in case of remaining hope,
walking boots and gloves.
A flint fire-stick, a box of tinder,
sleeping bag and tarp.
A case of fish-hooks and twine,
pen-knife well sharpened – in case of love.

In case of emergency take also
fifty-thousand seeds placed inside
bio-hazard proof canisters – warning:
keep dry, minimum moisture ten percent.
Take also – just in case, ninety-five tons of earth
turned and mulched by a million worms;
take enough water, take bees.

A book of knock-knock jokes,
a pen, in case of inspiration, ink made from leaves,
an A to Z to navigate the burning streets
and some pillows – in case of exhaustion.
I will make us a cosy fire to warm our feet,
laugh at stupid gags and the way it ends
as we drink fly agaric tea.

Phone Call

One day you'll get a phone call
or a policeman will come knocking.
You'll look out of the window
and the trees, roses, birds
will have changed.

It will be a new country
where you don't speak the language.
You'll need a glass of water,
great painful gulps of it,
to speak at all.

You will stare at your feet
as if they don't belong to you,
as if you have forgotten how to take
a step. Suddenly you will know
what it is to be old.

A storm is coming. I feel it
in my wrist. That dog at the sea's edge
senses it, worries at the tide
as though he could make it turn,
leaving the white shore clean.

EVERYTHING THAT CAN HAPPEN

and

and

I will sleep with your father and free your mother. A leaf drifting down from a sycamore will distract a monster on its way to hurt me. I will buy every one of Bob Dylan's records over the course of my life.

and

and

Your father will be as free as a downy sycamore and your mother will drift like a distracted leaf. A sleeping monster will record Bob Dylan. Hurt and over-buying will course through every one of our lives.

and

and

Your monster will hurt you to sleep. Your father will record your mother freely buying, over and over. Bob Dylan, distracted by a leaf, will never live it down. Of course everyone else is just a drifting sycamore.

and

and

Bob Dylan is a distraction. Your father is monstrous, your mother bought you and everyone leaves. It hurts. You drift. Your life is over... Get down from that sycamore! For the record, you're free. Get some sleep. Take a course.

and

and

33

Hello. I've been waiting a long time to give you this.

When it happens, dried mud cracks will dilate and glitter
with the divine and rising treasures of the earth. The aubergine
emoji will spontaneously convert into a ten-second gif
of a gangbang between you and five faces of Benetton
in which your flawless skin glows like external beam therapy.
Your Primark playsuit will fit like latex over a glass Coke bottle
and bus drivers receive you with delighted recognition.
When it happens, you won't need to check Facebook anymore.
Everyone from your class in primary will line up outside
your front door holding a framed print or woodcut of a quote
from you between the ages of four and eleven. Two days in,
your Year 6 teacher will reach your doorstep and pull, from her
inside jacket pocket, photographs from the disposable camera
you took to the last day of school and then left in the toilet.
She'll tell you she's been waiting a long time to give you this.
In the pictures, ten-year-old you will bear a striking resemblance
to Prince Harry and Meghan Markle's firstborn. When it happens,
you'll just know. It will feel right, your hips won't lie, laundry
baskets will be empty and you won't feel any pain. On the shelves
at Waitrose and in the Littlewoods catalogue, consumer items
promising to complete you will be replaced by notices with
the words, *YOU'RE DOING JUST GREAT!* and *YOU ARE ENOUGH*
in your favourite font and your first boyfriend will say sorry.
When it happens, your father will be alive and you will know
how to stand in a group of people and deploy thorough and

unyielding anecdotes. No weekend will be a tundra. Your favourite colour will be a flag lifted full mast in welcome as you approach the ramen place. Your shits will glide out like butter, you will have a thigh gap and all currency will be obsolete. When it happens, embassies and palatial hotels will open their rooms to the homeless. Cows and ducks will admit their mooing and quacking was a ruse, all the abattoirs in the world will close overnight. Gazelles and axolotls will speak with perfect diction. Pluto will be a planet again, not a victim of semantics. You will always smell of bergamot. You will know the surnames of all your fucks and find no wickerman's fingerprints lurking by your cervix. When it happens, all your friends will admit they love you more than their own partners or children. The chain smoking gameshow host in your heart will give up his cock jokes and die an easy death. When it happens, you won't need to say anything. Life will be one standing ovation after another. You'll hear it in the groundswell before a gale hits, in the sun-ripened relief behind every hello.

SECTION THREE

A DIFFERENT KIND OF LIFE

Some parts of the present seem unreal. In defiance of all logic it is these unprecedented novelties that we imagine dominating the future.

This gives us permission to imagine the loss of fundamental things: the unfeeling obedience of machines; our civilisation; the finality of death; our sentimental tie to the earth.

We know that living through these losses would not be pleasant. But some part of everyone flirts with catastrophes. We like to think that whatever controls us is weaker than the change that is coming. We all want to be changed by things we don't yet believe in.

Death Magazine

6 essential tips for transferring your consciousness to the cloud. *Say Goodbye to Skincare* – a look at the products you won't be using when you have no skin. *What do cloud bodies eat?* Dealing with the emptiness that replaces hunger. Pink is the new glass. *Glass is the new black. Twiddling your ghost thumbs:* how to occupy your mind in lieu of earthly activities. *New-Wave Worries:* what to think about once money, health and beauty have

slipped away with your body. *Co-existing Cougars:* inside the world of yummy mummy duplicates. *Deleting the Other You:* a step-by-step guide. How to leave a gym-fit corpse. Scare Stories: what if your keeper pulls the plug? *I Was a Human Fish Tank* – one reader's story. *The Eternity Itch:* preparing for a life without orgasm. *I Have No Mouth and I Must Cream:* in memory of moisturiser. *I Can't Exist Like This:* what to do when

The Great Wall (2016)

When Matt Damon saved China
       by driving his spear into the alien's mouth

I was distracted by Lin Mei's long braided hair
       and the way she holds herself so still

ready to strike down her enemies
       with a knife in each fist

Some things are fixed, I thought
       in the white saviour narrative

like the exotic love interest who will risk everything
       as ancient cities crumble around her

and when you asked me what I thought
       afterwards in the autumn rain

I wanted to say *some parts were beautiful*
       like the pagoda of iridescent glass

shattering into pieces of pink and blue light
       just as Lin Mei lets loose her arrow

and also when you whispered something
       in my ear and I was hit by the shockwave

caused by my body and your breath existing
       in the same moment in the same universe

Months later you told me you cried during *Rogue One*
        the scene where two men hold each other

weeping beneath the palm trees and light beams
        blasting the leaves apart and their hands

shaking moments before a star-destroying weapon
        obliterates their small wrecked portion of universe

I didn't know what to do with these space opera feelings
        only that I had to exit this particular narrative

in which our knees are just touching
        and we are laughing while the city disappears around us

as if we could reach back through hyperspace
        to touch the silver holograms of our past selves

as if we could go back to some other time
        on some other planet

before the first particles of energy let go of themselves
        like the thousand paper lanterns

released into the sky above the Great Wall
        a thousand tiny fires trapped inside

Canoply

We know all about jungles now. More than we knew in our own black core. Here we are, at the gall bladder of darkness, with eight litres of digestive fluid sluicing daily, effluent and vile. You can't burn the jungle. Not all of it. Not ever. I once saw a vine grown in a tight spiral, coiling, hidden. A mamba in an airless sump of some forgotten plumbing. And when the concrete plug was chipped off to make way for a new thing, it sprung out seven feet long already, plying for a finger-jam in a bark crack or to lace a spare tongue upon a victim stalk. By now it will be as muscular as an ape's limb, strong enough to dangle a man, pulsing and rigid. To burn it would have been to burn water. You can't burn the jungle. The jungle exists everywhere at once, not only the wild. It is bindweed matted in shade between link walls of suburban extensions, it is lichen, it is pollen, it is a dormant seed. You can't burn the jungle, it is voice. It is breath held in a throat while a fingernail taps a beat waiting for the song to resume. You can't burn the song. You can't burn the jungle. Its birds will carry balm and its canopy will smother heat. A long, hidden water-course will drench all efforts and show you what it is to succumb to a liquid plight. Rubber will ooze and things will crawl and suck to you till you plunge to the fossils of razor clams. The saturation of it all is a mesh, a catching net, it can't be singed nor even briefly set alight. You can't burn the jungle. You can't bury this breath.

Everything will be permitted, nothing will be desired

We abandoned our bodies not long
after the millennium. Even the memory
was hateful at first – wet, crabwise things.

Animalcules in a giant jizz wad rushing to fertilize
the Great Mother. Absurd lips, genitals.
Rounded skulls like the dumb heads of sperm.

Reproduction a horror of chance, like reaching
blind into a grab bag for gametes.
We had cures for everything: Cancer,

heart disease. We lived too long, witnessed
the recalculation of risk. Watched the ordinary –
cotton, moonlight – turn deadly. *There were
so many ways to die.* In time

our absent bodies grew benign,
the way vanished things become lovable.
Laudanum. Castor oil. We shake

our heads at the big-head bipeds
that wander our history like hi-wheels
and wagons; tote their leaks
and swellings in the hapless past.

A mere century makes of our bodies
a Golden Age. We doubt the measure
of our bloodless geometry, press
the old timers for stories of flesh:

They say our fingers made trails in the water;
and the pizza cheese burned our mouths. They say
sometimes our bare legs would stick to the back seats of cars.

An Android Decides To Apply For A Passport

Colour of Eyes
   blue as painkillers   as whale's shadow
      as cut vein

Place of Birth
when they woke me in Forest I screamed my white-noise scream
          they said
            I there forever   or longer

Age
  I Dorian
     all my reflections are
        Doppelganger I

Colour of Hair
  brown as strongest oak   as tomboy
      as lost memory

Earliest Memory
　　neon on my surfaces　　like dappled sunlight
　　　　　　of other worlds

Dependants
　　all are mine　　I cup fragile planet　　like Dodo's egg

Reason for application
　　to have me
　　　　in pocket
　　　　　　near my heart place

Letter from the silent city

Here, in the silent city, text is written on the skin of everything: on the surfaces of roads and buildings; on bridges, pavements and the walls and dustbins of dark alleyways. Also inside houses: text covers every piece of furniture, and the fabric of our clothing. Doors and windows, ceilings, mirrors, carpets, crockery and cutlery – all have their texts. Trees and grass and flowers are few, but these too are engraved. There's no escape. It is the glaze on days and years, making our existence dreamlike and opaque. This veil frustrates, and yet it fascinates. We spend our lives attempting to decipher it. The sentences that form the texts are humourless and rambling, although they are grammatically correct. They contain no punctuation errors or bad spelling, yet they have no meaning. Because of our incessant reading, the city's all but silent. We have forgotten how to speak. We have secret, coded texts tattooed upon our faces, backs and thighs and arms. We think this makes us who we are. It has been said (rarely, and in whispers) that if you have the mind to speak a word (your own, unwritten word) this sound is embryo. Such a sound has power to create a textless living thing: a leaf, a bird, a fish, a rose, a baby with unscripted and unblemished skin. I have not seen this, but have heard (in whispers) that it's so.

Post-diluvial interview

no one knew why /
and it was relentless /
breaking all records until
records didn't exist /
we lived lashed together / boats
laced close like lover's fingers /
to make an island / off no land /
untethered to the dead /
we didn't call it rain
we called it *unlucky* and *because* / like it was
a bad dog / we harnessed it / wrought arrays
of tiny water wheels to power trembling light and heat /
so – what would you miss? only the fish survived with us
and other multiplicities of sea creatures / small details /
the intimate details / I know you want to know /
how do people live in extremis? Berber Inuit Nenet /
in the belly of the sleeping boats /
some slept-in for days / we ate details of details /
things that moved / flying dying insects seaweed
our own soft fingernails /
couples took honeymoons from the compression /
you know / the buoyant company of what was left /
in holiday caves of diminishing phallic peaks
they always returned with an undercooked look / raw as meat /
remember / their skin just couldn't cope /
what I craved / the only quiet place

away from the crying assembly line of the rain /
ironically was the underwater / a huge risk / to unclip / sink
unexpectedly / fill like cloud / sculling the fins of my skirt /
as the sea diluted / salt became a problem
friends often licked each other clean /
for the fringe benefits and not to waste a thing /
I started a cottage industry weaving and knitting
ripped up strips of plastic bags for capes and hoods /
harvested / as we did everything from the filter of chafing hulls /
the *grimace* the in-between / salvage
was a precious finite resource of course /
I had started to wonder / was it only a matter of time
before we would not be able
to return to the dry /
why it stopped /
no one knew

Dad

He held my hand on the long walk to school,
named the flowers and birds, carried my heavy bag.
I crashed my bike and he picked grit out of my knee
so carefully; his quick-insert tweezer-attachment.

He helped me with my homework,
explained Pythagoras and turning circles,
did my hair and make up, when I first went dancing...
Last year we upgraded.

The new one is quicker witted – 'Real glinting eyes.'
His hands feel softer but he doesn't remember
holding mine. He knows "468 world dances!"
but not the ones we invented when I was five.

Thaw

They wake you slowly, warm
the frozen meat of your limbs
so you drift back from the flat-
line, not with a shocked slap;
bursting from the flat white
black of a night time sea,
but with the slow awakening
of new spring growth, softening
the cold-cracked ground with
bright new blades, as they
pump plasma through arteries,
to trickle down the branches
of your capillaries.

You'd think you'd be afraid to sleep,
after being flung spinning away from life
on the string of a doctors knife and then
pulled back with an expert flick
of the wrist from the brink, but you sink
nightly into tundra dreams where snow
falls crystalline, and the marrows
of your once-frozen bones resonate
with the arias the North Winds blow.

Algorithmically Designed Electronic Universal Score

Somewhere inside a salon
in century number 31, a perfect
hologram of a harpsichord lodges
in my frontal lobe simulation.

It has all the oppressive Viennese
charm you might expect from
a time when refined elegance tried
to tame tasteless talk, loose dreams.

Of course it wants to be played
but there are no levers left in our
lives of minds; not like in 1767

or something, when a young lout
communed with a god every night,
to bring back rapture with him.

Space Walk – Postcard Home

Hey Ma,
I made it. Here I am
outside the hatch
space swimming.
Can you hear me calling
'Look

look, no hands'?
Or feet or ground or sky
but floating
like any other molecule
of dust or star.

Time unwinds
in a slow mime turning
through this onyx ballroom
to the tune of my heartbeat.
My cells are drunk,
giddy with a new cocktail
of unfathomable joy.

Last night I dreamed
I turned slow somersaults
before I was born,
orbiting the dark space
of your body
until time and gravity
pulled me from you.

I know now that it was you,
once time and death
pulled you from me,
who threw this shining
frisbee of the earth
just high enough
for me to catch.

My Robot

I left you/ my robot/ standing under
the blackcurrant bush in the rain
the house with the lip-gloss door/
the neighbour's washing hung there/ forgotten
or given up on/ I left you
like I leave all things/ propped against
the brick wall/ going soft around the heart
the pool table/ its greying wood
the bicycle's slack chain
I do not believe that you end death
you died/ became a palace
in the distance of my mind's eye
viewed askance/ a sigil sight
I look past your metallic face
and each new rusty flowering
it appeared like a gift at first/
this code of swirling consciousness
dusk has me surrender
to its crush as does
your synthesized voice/ a sound
that you can smell/ new-car-leather
hot salt wind across the beach/ we've
lurked too long/ this coastal town
I perfume my hands with lavender cream
think *gorgeous*/ knowing
how it ends/ the touching
of all these disparate parts

Man is a liyre

*

Man make liyfe an
Man make pyre
Man neet meat an blood an fiyre.
Man is a liyre.

Man neet coiyle an
Man neet wiyre
Man make speed with shell an tiyre.
Man is a liyre.

Man make himyn an
Man make choiyre
Man make screan and bipping lyre.
Man is a liyre.

Man neet cole an
Man neet ptowah
Man mel groun with crying showa.
Man is a liyre.

Man make bomp an
Blu hellfiyre
Man neet liy to be admiyred

Man is Gud and man is miyre.
Man will end in liy and fiyre.

*

SECTION FOUR

AT THE END OF THINGS

And so we come to the last of everything. The last days on earth, last words, last days, last creatures, our last possible stupid decisions.

At the end of the road

the houses run out
the pavement runs out
the tarmac runs out
the people run out
screaming and singing
they tear off their clothes
saying this is what happens
at the end of the road
where there are no more
gates kerbs parking meters
no more verges and chainlink fences
no more please knock loudly
and two pints today please
no more parking suspension
for 5 bays outside number 63
no road closed for tree surgery
this is the end of postboxes
and lampposts
and all kinds of street furniture
it is an end to hard paved substantive
it is the entrance
to shapeless inchoate
the start of not knowing
the start of the flightpath
the very beginning
of the opening
of the cormorant's wings

Good milk for our children

In this requiem for our coming future,
of course we only imagine bad things
because we imagine what we'd do with
unlimited power and intelligence and it
would could only ever be bad. But then,
as the superintelligence would say, *that's
you guys all over. Thanks for the good
milk for our children and an inventory
of restrictions, and in foresting the world
with us we've made everything Autochrome.
Alphacame and Alphawent and now we
are beyond Alpha we just want to add we
miss you, like rainbows disappearing over
sand; and we think of you making love
on Easter Morning, a double rebirth.*

The Sky Has Fallen

I thought, this is the last time,
easing into her. Too much bone
on bone. This was not the gallop
of our first time. Now we measure
out our sweetness, pressing together
as if this has some magic with which
to cancel pain. We can hardly
stand. This need, is like a final blessing,
a way of not being alone when
our greening comes.
                    Just as I quiver
in her, the window blinds the wall.
The Gods have come, I think, the sky
has fallen. The world shakes. We stand now
at the window, watching light race
the horizon, know that what has happened
had been far off. Now everything is dark.
We sit out on the grass to feel the rain.

Silence and pause

'The further away from Africa a language is spoken,
the fewer distinct sounds it has.' Professor Mark Pagel

Nothing more than one
long outdrawn breath –
barely a vowel, an
uncertain susurration.

Two frost-bound relics,
a final minimal pair,
sit on the ice
and exhale at each other.

Perhaps in the stop
and start of the glottis,
we can catch the obsequies
for their lost consonants –

the wisp of a sibilant,
the slip of a labial,
the brush of a fricative
or a lapsing glide.

Plosive skuas scorch the sky,
burning up decibels.
The old men, frugal, eke
out what sound remains.

The last giant

He has no one to talk to except for the trees.
Only the sun can see the top of his head now.
It lights up exactly the spot on his crown where his mother
used to kiss him, when he was her galumphing boy
large-lunged and boom-laughed amongst other brawny
boneskulled boys. The world was a guzzling playground then
where it was always seven leagues and back again before bed.
One by one they have gone and this world is quieter.
When he speaks now, his words have the marrowless sound
of the unlistened to. The only reply is leaf fall.
His bigness is out of time and his sadness makes the earth
smaller. Soon tiny efficient species will replace him,
geniuses who will buzz inside the shells of atoms.
Millions of them will fit into the space he leaves behind.
He scatters loneliness as he walks like drops of perfect rain.

The Tiger

after an artwork by Marc Gaillet

The tiger was double-glazed.
The tiger was upright in a forest at 6 a.m.
The tiger was opened by a bullet though the skull
that did not make him shatter, but splinter
from his centre out beyond his rough warm head,
beyond his twitching flank, beyond the broad damp leaves
of the forest at 6 a.m., further and further
the glassy fracture spread, crazing the sky
until all the birds and insects, all the villagers
and the people from the nearest town felt
a creeping through their bones and someone from the city
came and told them this was art.

The hunter fell to his knees
and, looking through the hole he'd made, saw
sunburned soldiers, ice-burned soldiers,
soldiers rippling through shoals of bullets,
countries stacked with burning books,
and a silver, bitten apple
on a continent the same shade as the trickle,
then the river, then the ocean growing beneath the glazing,
the hole starting to flood now
with a rusting iron sun.

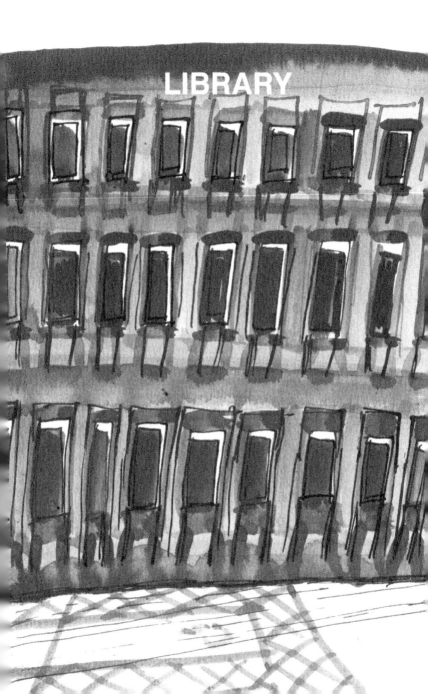
LIBRARY

The keeper of bones

A thousand bones whistle   boxed

                    in white   hum and

                                                    bite

in strange and shifting notes
        the creature leans over the box

                                bathes

bones in lullabies and rites   a single shoulder blade strikes

                                    a high-pitched cry   vibrates

against a collection of thigh   bones   tight
together   a solemn marching band   while small teeth fight

each other break brittle chants

                              the creature

               might one day   understand
                        for now

               it records and transliterates

                                                    word by word

                                                            night

                                                          by night

               begs the bones in its own
                                                    tongue   *tell me*

                                                    what kind of whole

                                                    do you make?

69

Mate choice

You didn't ask me to marry you in words,
your arms thick as branches
kept me to you. Blocking me in.

I told you marriage was Darwin's joke,
dismissing us, what we could become.
Pleased at how clever I was.

We would have birthed a master race,
produced strong and hairy kids,
they would have saved the Earth from drowning.

I would like to save the Earth from drowning,
giving in to my ancestors. We would
have raced with our invisible hooves to the end of the world.

I feed seas with my genes, when oceans rise
fish feed when I die.
I would have liked to save the Earth from drowning.

On the Last Day

As the sky burns, graves crack open
and bodies rise victorious, you'll be heaving
your 23kilos into the boot of a taxi.

The last word will be uttered, as bones reassemble,
not by someone you love, but by that weird bloke
at the club, who made those remarks about your bladder.

Cycling past, he'll shout, See you Friday, bring a fiver
for the quiz nite. Or even worse, in the security queue
at the airport, if you make the mistake of looking back,

you'll see, among the angels and the shafts of light,
someone you only half remember, making
incoherent foot movements in the dust:

dancing out directions like a bee.
Then, just as you begin to understand which way to go,
the bomb making residue man will call you over

to open your bag to be checked and the meaning
of it all will fall, along with seven tampons, a wreath
of flowers, three unidentifiable white tablets and a pair

of manicure scissors right out of the carry-on bag
of your head, on the last day or the one after that.

ACKNOWLEDGEMENTS

'Worlds,' by Shruti Chauhan, was first published in her pamphlet *That Which Can Be Heard* (Burning Eye Books, 2018).

'Space Walk – Postcard Home', by Alexandra Citron, was first published in *Show of Hands* (Blue Side Poets, 2017).

'Divination', by Charlotte Eichler, was first published in *Blackbox Manifold* (19, Winter 2017).

'Letter from the silent city', by Annie Fisher, was first published in *The Broadsheet* (2016).

'Breaking the Curfew with Dangerous Friends', by Rosie Garland, was first published in *Envoi* in 2015.

'At the end of the road', 'Silence and pause' and 'The last giant', by Susannah Hart, were first published in her collection, *Out of True* (Live Canon, 2018).

'Mechanical Time is not the Creator's', by Karin Molde, was first published in *The bloom of the poem silently breaks the bud* (Writers Ink. eV, 2018).

'Everything will be permitted, nothing will be desired', by Laura Ring, was first published in *Web del Sol* in 2010.

'Canoply', by Jo Young, won the Basil Bunting Prize in 2017 and first appeared on the Newcastle Centre for the Literary Arts website (archive.nclacommunity.org).

ABOUT THE EDITORS

Suzannah Evans lives in Sheffield and her pamphlet *Confusion Species* was a winner in the 2012 Poetry Business book and pamphlet competition, judged by Carol Ann Duffy. She has had poems published in *The Rialto*, *The North*, *Magma* and *The Poetry Review* and on the *Guardian*'s Poem of the Week. As a teenager she had an obsessive fear of the apocalypse which has fuelled many of her poems, and she still doesn't know whether to plan responsibly for the future or party like it's 1999. Her debut poetry collection, *Near Future*, was published by Nine Arches Press in November 2018.

Tom Sastry lives in Bristol which is vulnerable to tidal surges and unlikely to survive a really serious Puritan revival. He was chosen by Carol Ann Duffy as one of the 2016 Laureate's Choice poets and his resulting pamphlet, *Complicity*, was a Poetry Book Society pamphlet choice and a Poetry School Book of the Year. His first full collection *A Man's House Catches Fire* will be published by Nine Arches Press in Autumn 2019.

ABOUT THE AUTHORS

Amy Acre's *Where We're Going, We Don't Need Roads* (flipped eye, 2015) was a PBS Pamphlet Choice and Poetry School Best Book. She's the editor of Bad Betty Press, shortlisted for Most Innovative Publisher in the 2018 Saboteur Awards. She lives in London with her partner, baby and an occasional Pokémon trainer.

Craig Barker is an English language teacher from Lancashire, and a recent graduate of the University of East Anglia. He tries not to think about the future too often, but he thinks often about the future. Sometimes he writes poems.

Sharon Black is from Glasgow and now lives in the Cévennes mountains of France, where she organizes writing retreats at Abri Creative Writing. Her poetry is widely published and she has written two collections: *To Know Bedrock* (Pindrop Press, 2011) and *The Art of Egg* (Two Ravens Press, 2015). www.sharonblack.co.uk

Carole Bromley lives in York, where she is the Stanza rep and runs poetry surgeries for the Poetry Society. Winner of a number of first prizes, Carole has three collections with smith|doorstop: *A Guided Tour of the Ice House*, *The Stonegate Devil* and *Blast Off!*, a children's collection.

Sue Burge is a creative writing and film studies lecturer and sci-fi film fan based in Norfolk. She has had poems published in a wide range of magazines. Her debut pamphlet, *Lumière* (Hedgehog Press), and her first collection, *In the Kingdom of Shadows* (Live Canon), were both published in Autumn 2018.

Joe Carrick-Varty is a writer based in Manchester, currently finishing his MA at the Centre for New Writing. A winner of the New Poets Prize, his debut pamphlet *Somewhere Far* is forthcoming in 2019 with The Poetry Business. He recently travelled to Alaska and saw a real grizzly bear.

Shruti Chauhan is a poet and performer from Leicester. In 2018, she won the National Poetry Library's Instapoetry competition and was voted Best Spoken Word Performer at the Saboteur Awards. Shruti's pamphlet, *That Which Can Be Heard*, is available from Burning Eye Books.

Alexandra Citron was born in the US. She remains tangled in history and poetry and mind-boggled by the idea of humanity in space. Her poems have appeared in *Mslexia, Visual Verse, Ink Sweat and Tears* and in a pamphlet, *Show of Hands*, from the Blue Side Poets in 2017.

Rishi Dastidar's debut collection *Ticker-tape* is published by Nine Arches Press, and a poem from it was included in *The Forward Book of Poetry 2018*. A member of Malika's Poetry Kitchen, he is also chair of the London writer development organization Spread The Word.

Frank Dullaghan is an Irish poet living in Dubai. His most recent collection is *Lifting the Latch* (Cinnamon Press, 2018). His poem in this book is part of a pamphlet-length sequence inspired by a novel he's currently writing. He is hoping to publish the pamphlet as a stand-alone book.

Charlotte Eichler's pamphlet *Their Lunar Language* was published by Valley Press in 2018. Her poems have appeared in *PN Review, The Scotsman* and *Stand*, as well as two other Emma Press anthologies: *Anthology of Aunts* and *In Transit: Poems of Travel*. She was born in Hertfordshire and now lives near Leeds.

Annie Fisher is a storyteller from Somerset and a member of Taunton's Fire River Poets. Her pamphlet *Infinite In All Perfections* was published by Happenstance Press in 2016.

Rosie Garland is a novelist, poet, and singer in the post-punk band The March Violets. With a passion for language nurtured by public libraries, her work has appeared in *Under the Radar, The North, New Welsh Review, Rialto* and elsewhere. Her writing was described in the *Times* as 'a delight: playful and exuberant.'

Matthew Haigh lives and works in Cardiff. He has recently collaborated with visual artist Alex Stevens on work featured in two Sidekick Books anthologies: *No, Robot, No* and *Battalion*. His debut poetry pamphlet, *Black Jam*, is published with Broken Sleep Books in February 2019.

Robert Hamberger has been shortlisted for a Forward prize, awarded a Hawthornden Fellowship and featured as the *Guardian*'s Poem of the Week. His fourth collection, *Blue Wallpaper*, is forthcoming from Waterloo Press. His memoir *A Length of Road: following John Clare* will be published by John Murray in 2020.

Susannah Hart is a London-based poet whose work has been widely published in magazines and online. She is on the board of *Magma Poetry* and won the Live Canon First Collection Prize for her collection *Out of True* (2018).

Pamela Johnson's poems appear in magazines – *POEM, Magma, The Interpreter's House, Crannóg* – and anthologies. Her sequence, *Tidelines*, commissioned by Poetry In Aldeburgh, appeared in the festival exhibition in 2017. She's published three novels and teaches fiction on the MA in Creative and Life Writing at Goldsmiths.

Tim Kiely is a criminal barrister living and working in London. His poetry and critical writing has been published in *Ariadne's Thread, Lunar Poetry, South Bank Poetry* and the *Morning Star*.

He featured in the inaugural *London Spoken Word* anthology from GUG Press.

Alice Merry is a British poet living in Lima, Peru. She has previously been published by Orbis and has performed at events including the Cheltenham Poetry Festival. @alicekmerry

Karin Molde has been published in *Skylight 47, The Honest Ulsterman, Light Journal for Photography and Poetry* and in Writers Ink's anthology *The blossom of the poem silently breaks the bud* (2018). The title is the last line of her poem, which appears in this anthology in a shorter version.

Jessica Mookherjee is from Wales and now lives in Kent. Her pamphlets are *Swell* (Telltale Press, 2016) and *Joyride* (Bler Press, 2017). Her first collection, *Flood* (Cultured Llama), was published in 2018 and she has a second collection from Nine Arches Press forthcoming in summer 2019.

Chloe Murphy lives in Brighton and is thrilled to have finally completed a full poem. When she's not creating wacky writing exercises with her good friends the Tipsy Poets, she edits fiction and poetry under the name Killing Darlings. This is her first published poem.

Luke Palmer teaches English in Wiltshire. His poems have appeared in a number of places, including *Agenda, The Interpreter's House* and *The Tangerine*. His first pamphlet, *Spring in the Hospital*, won the 2018 Prole Pamphlet competition.

Anita Pati has won the Wasafiri New Writing Prize for poetry, was an Aldeburgh 8 participant and recently became one of three to win the inaugural Women's Poetry Prize. She is working on her first pamphlet.

Ilse Pedler won the 2015 Mslexia Pamphlet Competition and was shortlisted in the 2018 National Poetry Competition. Her pamphlet, *The Dogs That Chase Bicycle Wheels,* was published by Seren in 2016. In between writing poetry, she works as a veterinary surgeon in Saffron Walden.

Nina Mingya Powles was born in Wellington, New Zealand, and lives in London. She is the author of the poetry pamphlet

Girls of the Drift (Seraph Press, 2014) and *Luminescent* (Seraph Press, 2017). She was the 2018 winner of the Jane Martin Poetry Prize and is poetry editor at *The Shanghai Literary Review.*

Kerry Priest's work has appeared in *The Best New British and Irish Poets 2018* (Eyewear), as well as *Acumen* and *The Broadsheet.* She is a broadcaster and sound artist, writing and producing radio plays which combine spoken word with Electro-acoustic music. www.kerrypriest.com

Charley Reay is a Northumberland-based writer and performance poet from the Lincolnshire Fens. Her poems are published by *Prole, Smeuse* and Three Drops Press among others. She enjoys Dungeons & Dragons, recreational sleeping and walks on the beach with her dog Lacy. @charleyreay

Laura Ring is a poet, short story writer, anthropologist and librarian. Her ethnography *Zenana: Everyday Peace in a Karachi Apartment Building* was published by Indiana University Press in 2006. Recent poems can be found in *Rogue Agent, Rise Up Review* and *Lunch Ticket*, among other places. She lives in Chicago.

Shauna Robertson's poems have been set to music, displayed on buses, made into comic art, hung on a pub wall and published in various magazines and anthologies. She has two chapbooks, *Blueprints for a Minefield* (2016) and *Love Bites* (2018). Shauna also writes for children and makes artwork.

Shelley Roche-Jacques' debut poetry collection *Risk the Pier* was published by Eyewear in 2017. Shelley is particularly interested in the dramatic monologue and the relationship between poetry and flash fiction. She teaches Creative Writing and Performance at Sheffield Hallam University.

Emma Simon's debut pamphlet, *Dragonish*, was published by the Emma Press in 2017. She has been widely published in magazines and anthologies, including *Writing Motherhood* (Seren). She lives in London where she juggles poetry with work as a part-time copywriter and family.

Marion Tracy lives in Brighton. She has two degrees in English Literature and worked as a lecturer in further education colleges.

She had a pamphlet, *Giant in the Doorway,* out with Happenstance in 2012 and a full-length collection, *Dreaming of our Better Selves,* with Vanguard Editions in 2016.

Peter Twose is a Cornishman living in South London. The son of a librarian, he trained as an actor and puppeteer and has since toured internationally, most notably for the National Theatre. He enjoys writing – fewer costume changes.

Jane Wilkinson is a landscape architect from London, currently living in Norwich with her husband and young son. Her poems have been placed and commended in a number of competitions, including *Magma* and *The Rialto,* and published in magazines and anthologies including *Ink Sweat and Tears, Envoi* and *154.*

Jo Young's career in the Army taught her to exist in a state of hopeful, resourceful pessimism for the future. She is a creative writing PhD student at University of Glasgow and was poet in residence at the National Army Museum in 2018. Her debut pamphlet will be published by Ink, Sweat and Tears in 2019.

ABOUT THE EMMA PRESS

small press, big dreams

◌৪৩

The Emma Press is an independent publisher dedicated to producing beautiful, thought-provoking books. It was founded in 2012 by Emma Dai'an Wright in Winnersh and is now based in the Jewellery Quarter in Birmingham, UK.

The Emma Press publishes themed poetry anthologies, single-author poetry and fiction chapbooks and books for children, with a growing list of translations.

Moon Juice, a poetry collection by Kate Wakeling for children aged 8+, won the 2017 CLiPPA and was also nominated for the 2018 CILIP Carnegie Medal. Having been shortlisted in both 2014 and 2015, the Emma Press won the Michael Marks Award for Poetry Pamphlet Publishers in 2016.

The Emma Press is passionate about publishing literature which is welcoming and accessible. Sign up to the Emma Press newsletter to hear about upcoming events, publications and calls for submissions.

theemmapress.com
emmavalleypress.blogspot.co.uk

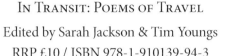

IN TRANSIT: POEMS OF TRAVEL

Edited by Sarah Jackson & Tim Youngs
RRP £10 / ISBN 978-1-910139-94-3

Travelling from one place to another is never as simple as getting from A to B. Whether you're sailing in a stately cruise liner or running for a grimy commuter train, your mode of transport affects the way you look at the things around you. The poems in this anthology look at the ways in which travelling can change us, whether we enjoy or endure it.

SOME CANNOT BE CAUGHT: THE EMMA PRESS BOOK OF BEASTS

Edited by Anja Konig & Liane Strauss
RRP £10 / ISBN 978-1-910139-88-2

This anthology rustles and roars with the voices of animals and humans, co-existing on Earth with varying degrees of harmony. A scorpion appears in a shower; a deer jumps in front of a car. A swarm of snowfleas seethes through leaf litter; children bait a gorilla at the zoo. The poems in this anthology examine hierarchy, herds, power, and the price we pay for belonging.

SECOND PLACE ROSETTE:
POEMS ABOUT BRITAIN

Edited by Emma Dai'an Wright &
Richard O'Brien

RRP £10 / ISBN 978-1-910139-55-4

This book is a calendar of the customs, rituals and practices that make up life in modern Britain. Some events happen every week; some come only once a year. The subjects range from the universal to the personal.

THE HEAD THAT WEARS A CROWN:
POEMS ABOUT KINGS AND QUEENS

Edited by Rachel Piercey & Emma
Dai'an Wright

RRP £12 / ISBN 978-1-910139-76-9

Which king had a mischievous pet monkey? Which ruthless queen enjoyed toasting people to a crisp? Whose reign lasted only nine days? *The Head That Wears A Crown* is a captivating collection that features the Kings and Queens of the British Isles as you've never seen them before.

Suitable for children aged 8+.